kenny chesney
when the sun goes down

ISBN 0-634-07973-5

HAL•LEONARD® CORPORATION
7777 W. BLUEMOUND RD. P.O. BOX 13819 MILWAUKEE, WI 53213

THERE GOES MY LIFE

Words and Music by WENDELL MOBLEY
and NEIL THRASHER

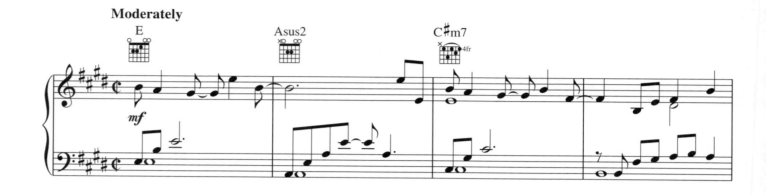

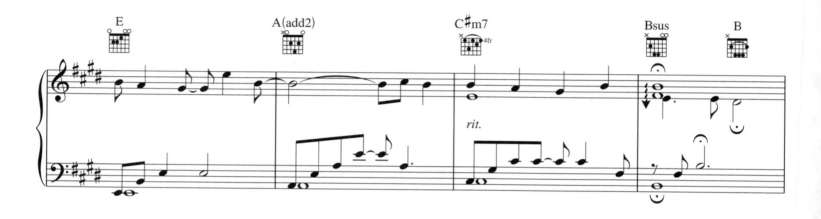

I GO BACK

Words and Music by
KENNY CHESNEY

ty yard line, __ a blan - ket, a girl, __ some rasp - ber - ry wine, __
fade to fall, __ grow-ing up __ too __ fast __ and I do __ re - call __

wish - ing time __ would stop __ right in its tracks. __

Ev -'ry time I hear that __ song, __ I go __ back, __

I go __ back. __

WHEN THE SUN GOES DOWN

Words and Music by
BRETT JAMES

sun goes _ down.

THE WOMAN WITH YOU

Words and Music by DAVID RAY FRASIER
and CRAIG WISEMAN

She hit the door, _ six - fif - ty - five, _ sack full of gro - ceries
girl I _ was _ with the busi - ness de - gree _ prob - 'ly would - n't

SOME PEOPLE CHANGE

Words and Music by MICHAEL DULANEY,
JASON SELLERS and NEIL THRASHER

ANYTHING BUT MINE

Words and Music by
SCOOTER CARUSOE

ev - er ___ be   an - y - thing ___ but ___

mine.   There's a

mine. *Guitar solo*

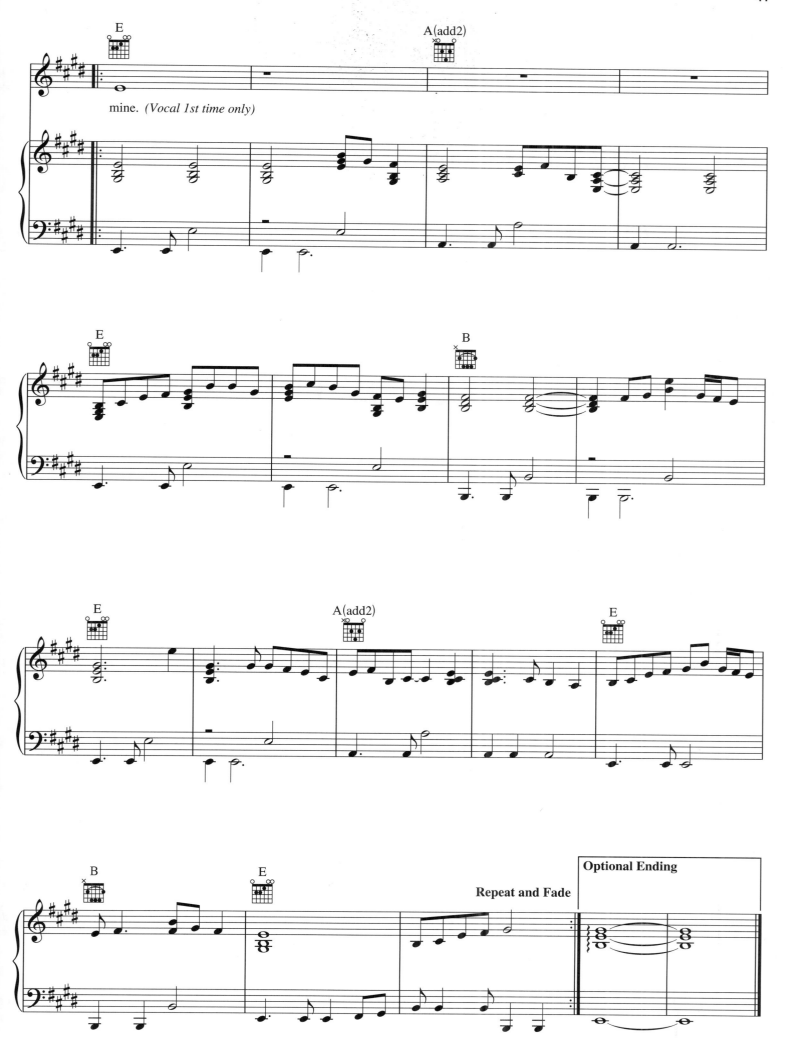

mine. *(Vocal 1st time only)*

KEG IN THE CLOSET

Words and Music by KENNY CHESNEY
and BRETT JAMES

Moderately fast

We had a dog __ named Bo- se- fus liv- ing in the front yard. __ He liked

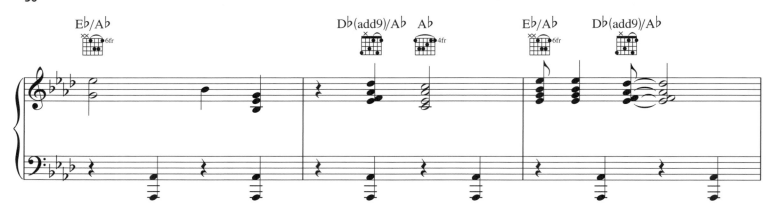

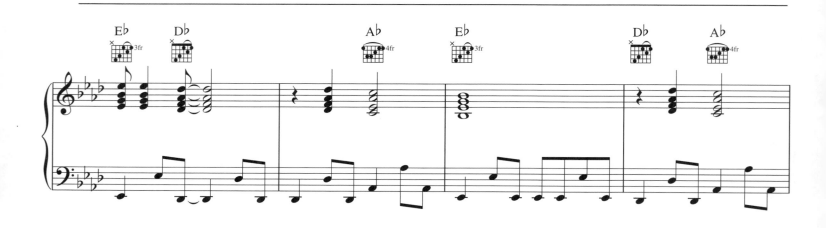

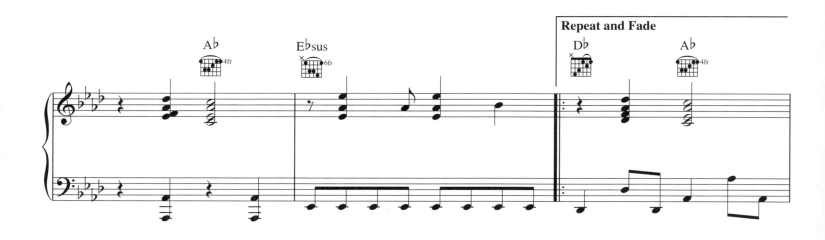

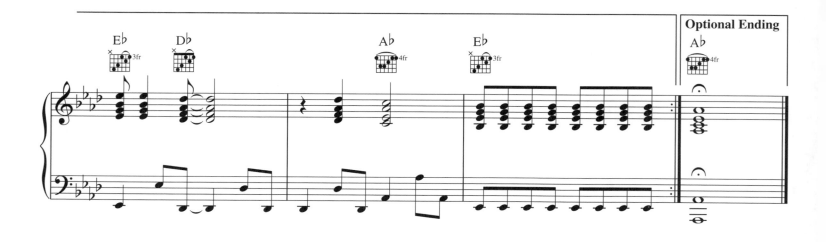

WHEN I THINK ABOUT LEAVING

Words and Music by TIMOTHY JON JOHNSON,
RORY LEE and PAUL OVERSTREET

Spoken: *You know, sometimes me and my lady have these crazy thoughts.*
Spoken: *You know, I got a friend and him and his wife just couldn't see eye to eye.*
And when we do, it makes me

wonder if we're ever gonna get it right.
He had all he could stand one day and just packed up and said, "Goodbye."
When I think a-bout ___
When I think a-bout ___

Spoken: *I never will forget her face or the day she told me about her dad,* *how he walked out on her and her mom*

when she was just a kid.

When I think a - bout leav - ing, leav - ing,

oh, I think a - bout her, on - ly five years old and her

oh, I think a - gain, _____ e - ven though that thought cross - es my ___

heart filled up with hurt, _____
mind ev-'ry now and then. _____

with her lit-tle arms ____wrapped a-round his
In my heart I know _____ I would nev-er

neck, say-ing, "Dad-dy, where you go-ing? Are you com-ing back?" ____ When I think a-bout
leave, there's no-where else on earth __ that I ____ would rath-er be. When I think a-bout

To Coda

leav-ing, oh, I think a-bout her.
leav-ing,

Spoken: You know, truth is, most of the time things were really great.

BEING DRUNK'S A LOT LIKE LOVING YOU

Words and Music by KENNY CHESNEY
and SKIP EWING

OUTTA HERE

Words and Music by
JOSH LEO

(Vocal 1st time only)

Repeat and Fade

Optional Ending

OLD BLUE CHAIR

Words and Music by
KENNY CHESNEY

Original key: F# major. This edition has been transposed down one half-step to be more playable.